I0824861

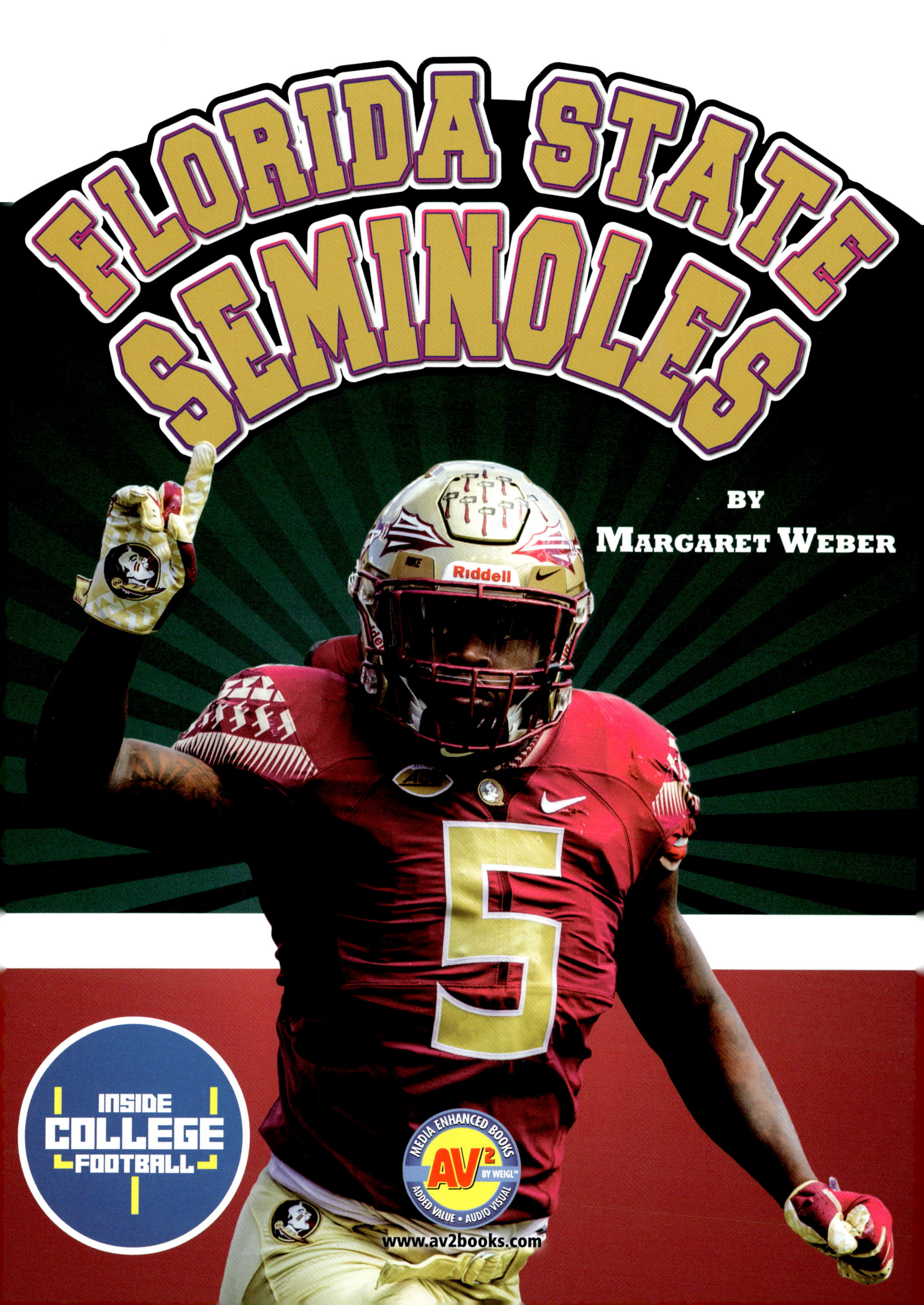
FLORIDA STATE SEMINOLES
BY
MARGARET WEBER
INSIDE
COLLEGE
FOOTBALL
MEDIA ENHANCED BOOKS
AV2
BY WEIGL
ADDED VALUE • AUDIO VISUAL
www.av2books.com

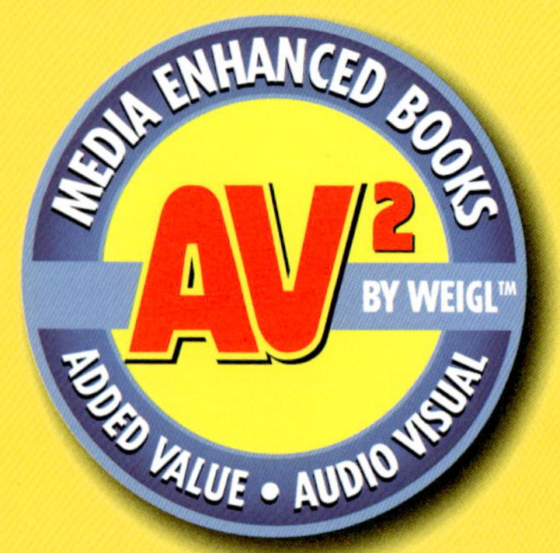

Go to www.av2books.com, and enter this book's unique code.

BOOK CODE

AVV95832

AV² by Weigl brings you media enhanced books that support active learning.

AV² provides enriched content that supplements and complements this book. Weigl's AV² books strive to create inspired learning and engage young minds in a total learning experience.

Your AV² Media Enhanced books come alive with...

Audio
Listen to sections of the book read aloud.

Video
Watch informative video clips.

Embedded Weblinks
Gain additional information for research.

Try This!
Complete activities and hands-on experiments.

Key Words
Study vocabulary, and complete a matching word activity.

Quizzes
Test your knowledge.

Slideshow
View images and captions, and prepare a presentation.

... and much, much more!

Published by AV² by Weigl
350 5th Avenue, 59th Floor
New York, NY 10118
Website: www.av2books.com

Library of Congress Control Number: 2018968219

ISBN 978-1-7911-0105-3 (hardcover)
ISBN 978-1-7911-0106-0 (multi-user eBook)
ISBN 978-1-7911-0107-7 (single-user eBook)

Printed in Guangzhou, China
1 2 3 4 5 6 7 8 9 0 23 22 21 20 19

042019
102318

Project Coordinator: Jared Siemens   Designer: Terry Paulhus

Every reasonable effort has been made to trace ownership and to obtain permission to reprint copyright material. The publishers would be pleased to have any errors or omissions brought to their attention so that they may be corrected in subsequent printings.

The publisher acknowledges Alamy, Getty Images, Newscom, and Wikimedia Commons as its primary image suppliers for this title.

Florida State Seminoles

CONTENTS

Introduction

The Seminoles represent Florida State University in the National Collegiate Athletic Association (NCAA) Division 1 Football Bowl Subdivision (FBS). Since 1947, the Seminoles have evolved into one of college football's strongest teams. Known for its unique traditions and multiple titles, including 3 National Championships and 18 conference titles, Florida State is a dynamic team that plays to win. The Seminoles have dominated their biggest **rivals** in recent seasons, including in-state rivals the University of Miami Hurricanes and the Florida State Gators.

Many Seminoles players have earned national recognition and have played professional football. Around 40 FSU players were named consensus **All-Americans**, and more than 250 Seminoles have played in the National Football League (NFL). The **Fred Biletnikoff Award** was named for a former Florida State player, and three **Heisman Memorial Trophy** winners played for the Seminoles.

Running back Cam Akers was the Seminoles' leading rusher in the 2017 season with 1,024 yards, a Florida State freshman rushing record.

Some of college football's most legendary coaches have led the Seminoles. The team holds records for consecutive winning seasons and bowl game appearances, and three FSU teams in the school's history played perfect seasons. Current coach Willie Taggart has his sights set on continuing the Seminoles' winning traditions.

Kicker Ricky Aguayo has made 123 out of his 126 extra points attempted for Florida State. Aguayo has scored 267 points for the Seminoles over three seasons.

FLORIDA STATE

Stadium Doak Campbell Stadium

Division Atlantic Coast Conference (ACC) Atlantic

Head Coach Willie Taggart

Location Tallahassee, Florida

National Championships 3

Nicknames Florida State, FSU, Seminoles, Noles

2 Home Stadiums

15 Conference Titles

264 Players Drafted into the NFL

218 All-American Players

History

Florida State had its **first win** over a Southeastern Conference (SEC) opponent in **1958**, when it beat Tennessee 10–0.

Bobby Bowden had planned to spend only a few seasons at Florida State. He retired from coaching having completed 34 seasons with the Seminoles.

The first college football team in Florida began in 1902 at Florida State College in Tallahassee, Florida. That football team was known simply as the Eleven, because it had no formal nickname. They only played until 1904, when reorganization of the college system changed Florida State College to the Florida State College for Women.

The Seminoles team began again when more changes were made to the Florida college system. Many colleges in Florida merged in order to accommodate veterans returning from World War II (1939–1945). In 1947, the Florida State College for Women became Florida State University. Ed Williamson became the first coach of the Florida Seminoles. He is often given credit for bringing football back to the college.

By the 1960s, the Florida State Seminoles were starting to gain national attention. They began to post winning seasons and appeared in bowl games four times between 1960 and 1970. By 1976, when Bobby Bowden stepped into the role of head coach, they were ready to become a truly competitive team. Bowden finished his first season as coach with a losing record, but would go on to be the winningest coach in Seminoles history. This era of wins and championships is remembered as one of the greatest periods in all of college football history.

The first Florida State team, known as the Florida State College Eleven, wore gold uniforms with a large purple F on the front.

The Stadium

Known to fans as "Doak," Florida State's Doak Campbell Stadium is the second-largest in the ACC.

Doak Campbell Stadium is home to Bobby Bowden Field and the Florida State Seminoles. It is named for Doak S. Campbell, who was president of the college in the 1940s and 1950s. The stadium hosted its first football game in 1950.

Known as "the House that Bobby built," the stadium is the largest continuous brick structure in the United States. Florida State fans are known for their loud cheers and songs. Attending a game at Doak Campbell Stadium includes more than just football. Fireworks are launched from the north side of the stadium throughout the game to celebrate the Seminoles. The Florida State marching band often plays before the game and during halftime, entertaining fans and cheering on the team.

The stadium has gone through several expansions and upgrades since it was built. Seating capacity was increased for the first time in 1954, and again in 2003, when the capacity was raised to 82,300. The most recent **renovation** in 2016 added new scoreboards and reduced the stadium's seating capacity to 79,560. Florida State continues to make improvements to the stadium, including the addition of an indoor practice field.

Outside Doak Campbell Stadium's south entrance, a statue called Unconquered features Osceola and Renegade, Florida State's horse-and-rider mascots.

Where They Play

Welcome to Bobby Bowden Field at Doak Campbell Stadium, home of the Florida State University Seminoles. Nearly 80,000 fans dressed in garnet and gold fill "the house that Bobby built" to watch the Seminoles dominate their opponents. FSU's horse and rider charge the field while the Marching Chiefs play the Florida State fight song. Beautiful architecture and honored traditions mix with a spirit of winning on game days at Doak Campbell Stadium.

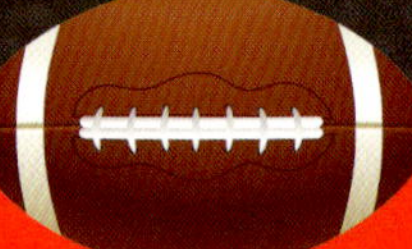

ACC ATLANTIC

1. **Boston College**
   Chestnut Hill, Massachusetts
2. **Clemson University**
   Clemson, South Carolina
3. ★ **Florida State University**
   Tallahassee, Florida
4. **North Carolina State University**
   Raleigh, North Carolina
5. **Syracuse University**
   Syracuse, New York
6. **University of Louisville**
   Louisville, Kentucky
7. **University of Notre Dame**
   Notre Dame, Indiana
8. **Wake Forest University**
   Winston-Salem, North Carolina

Arena
Doak Campbell Stadium

Location
Tallahassee, Florida

Broke Ground
June 1950

Completed
October 1950

Surface
Real Grass

Features
- The scoreboard in the north end zone is more than 60 feet (18 meters) high
- A three-story stained glass window depicts the naming of the field over one entrance
- There is a bronze statue depicting a family of Seminole people outside the stadium

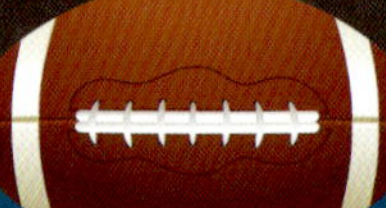

ACC COASTAL

1. **Duke University**
   Durham, North Carolina
2. **Georgia Institute of Technology**
   Atlanta, Georgia
3. **University of Miami**
   Coral Gables, Florida
4. **University of North Carolina at Chapel Hill**
   Chapel Hill, North Carolina
5. **University of Pittsburgh**
   Pittsburgh, Pennsylvania
6. **University of Virginia**
   Charlottesville, Virginia
7. **Virginia Polytechnic Institute and State University**
   Blacksburg, Virginia

NORTH DAKOTA
SOUTH DAKOTA
MINNESOTA
WISCONSIN
MICHIGAN
NEBRASKA
IOWA
ILLINOIS
INDIANA
OHIO
KANSAS
MISSOURI
KENTUCKY
OKLAHOMA
ARKANSAS
TENNESSEE
TEXAS
LOUISIANA
MISSISSIPPI
ALABAMA
GEORGIA
FLORIDA
SOUTH CAROLINA
NORTH CAROLINA
VIRGINIA
WEST VIRGINIA
PENNSYLVANIA
NEW YORK
NEW JERSEY
DELAWARE
MARYLAND
WASHINGTON, D.C.
CONNECTICUT
RHODE ISLAND
MASSACHUSETTS
VERMONT
NEW HAMPSHIRE
MAINE
1
2
3
4
5
6
7
8
1
2
3
4
5
6
7
Atlantic Ocean
Gulf of Mexico
N
S
E
W
SCALE
0 miles
500 miles
0 kilometers
500 km
LEGEND
Home Stadium
ACC Atlantic
ACC Coastal
United States
Other Countries
Water

The Uniforms

The Seminoles' arrow helmet was designed by **Coach Bobby Bowden** and actor **Burt Reynolds,** with the help of a Hollywood costume designer.

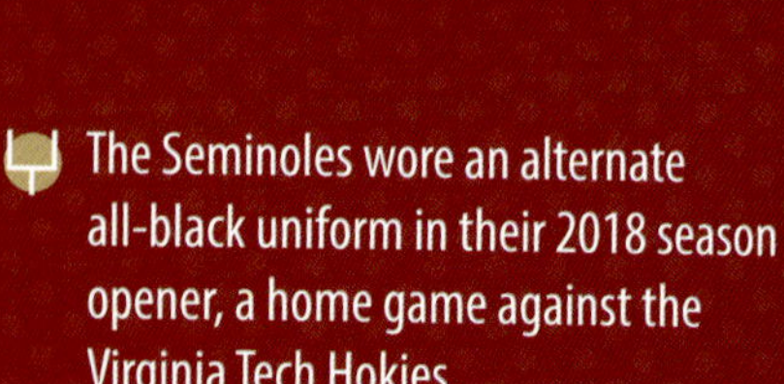

The Seminoles wore an alternate all-black uniform in their 2018 season opener, a home game against the Virginia Tech Hokies.

The Seminoles play in the colors garnet and gold. Garnet is a particular shade of red. These colors were first adopted in 1904. They were worn by the original Seminoles. While there have been changes to the uniforms and helmets throughout the years, these colors have remained consistent.

The home uniforms of the Seminoles have garnet jerseys, gold pants, and gold helmets. When the team is away, players wear white uniforms that are accented with garnet sleeves and garnet numbers. They wear their gold helmets in every game.

The actor Burt Reynolds was an alumnus of Florida State University and often was involved in updating the appearance of the team's uniforms. His influence was one reason the Seminoles brought white pants back to the uniform in 1988. Reynolds had worn them in the 1950s when he played for the team.

Florida State players earn tomahawk helmet decals for performance on the field and in the classroom. They can also have the decals taken away for poor decisions during games. Athletes who earn top accomplishments in their classes receive tomahawks with "academic" written on the handle.

Student Athletes

Four graduates of **IMG Academy**, a training academy for high school athletes, have gone on to play **football** for the Seminoles.

Running back Jacques Patrick rushed for 1,790 yards in 37 games for the Seminoles from 2015 to 2018.

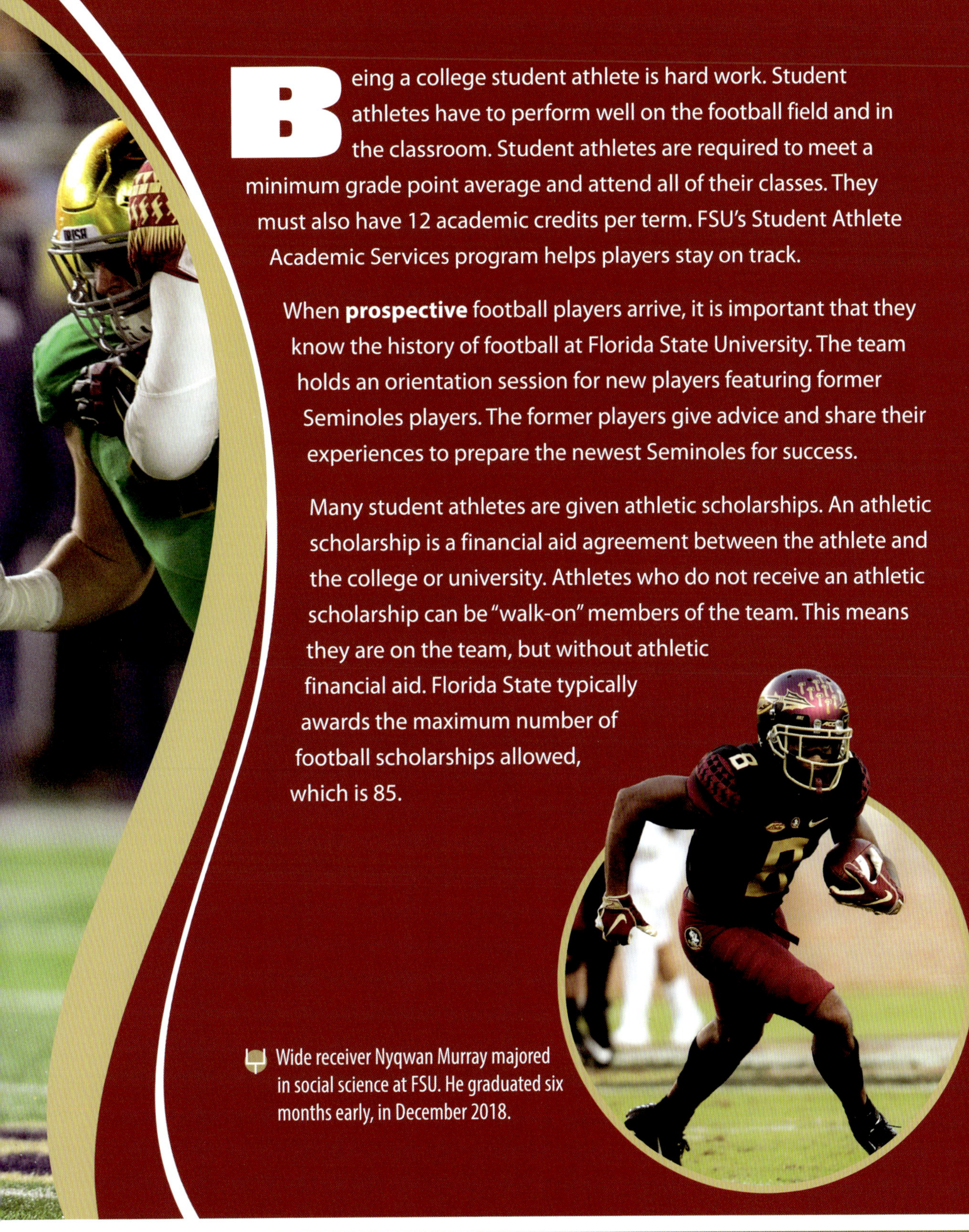

Being a college student athlete is hard work. Student athletes have to perform well on the football field and in the classroom. Student athletes are required to meet a minimum grade point average and attend all of their classes. They must also have 12 academic credits per term. FSU's Student Athlete Academic Services program helps players stay on track.

When **prospective** football players arrive, it is important that they know the history of football at Florida State University. The team holds an orientation session for new players featuring former Seminoles players. The former players give advice and share their experiences to prepare the newest Seminoles for success.

Many student athletes are given athletic scholarships. An athletic scholarship is a financial aid agreement between the athlete and the college or university. Athletes who do not receive an athletic scholarship can be "walk-on" members of the team. This means they are on the team, but without athletic financial aid. Florida State typically awards the maximum number of football scholarships allowed, which is 85.

Wide receiver Nyqwan Murray majored in social science at FSU. He graduated six months early, in December 2018.

Bowl Games

Between 1985 and 1996, the Seminoles won **11 straight** bowl games.

The Seminoles have won 62 percent of the bowl games they have played. FSU's most recent bowl win was the 2017 Independence Bowl, a 42–13 defeat of the University of Southern Mississippi Golden Eagles.

Bowl games are a unique sports tradition in college football. In the beginning of college football, there was no true **postseason**. Today, a variety of postseason bowl games are played. Bowl games give teams the opportunity to continue striving for recognition and victory after the end of regular play. There are currently 40 bowl games played in various combinations each year.

The Florida State Seminoles are used to appearing in the **off-season**. They have played in a total of 47 bowl games. The Seminoles have made the most appearances in the Orange Bowl, which they have played 10 times. In 2017, Florida State played the University of Southern Mississippi in the Independence Bowl. This marked their 36th consecutive appearance in a bowl game. However, the NCAA does not officially recognize this bowl record. The team's 2006 Emerald Bowl record was **vacated** due to an academic cheating scandal.

Quarterback Deondre Francois rushed for a touchdown during the fourth quarter of the 2016 Orange Bowl. Francois helped the Seminoles secure a 33–32 victory over the University of Michigan Wolverines.

The Coaches

Bobby Bowden led the Seminoles to 2 National Championships, 12 ACC titles, and 31 bowl games.

There have been 13 head coaches for the Florida State Seminoles since 1902. Of those, 11 have served since 1947, which is considered the modern era of Seminoles football. Each of these coaches has left a mark on the team, although none has been greater than that of Bobby Bowden. His legacy is one each coach can draw on for inspiration for the future of the Seminoles.

BOBBY BOWDEN Despite impressive offers from other teams, including one from the NFL, Bobby Bowden stayed with the Seminoles for 34 years, from 1976 to 2009. His final record was 315–97–4. The NCAA recognizes him as the second-winningest coach in all of college football, behind Joe Paterno. He has been the greatest coach in Florida State history.

BILL PETERSON Bill Peterson coached the Florida Seminoles for 11 seasons, from 1960 to 1970. He is seen as a unique coach in college football history who was not afraid to try new things with his team. He brought pro-style passing to the Seminoles. He was also the first to recruit African American players for the team. Peterson was the first coach to lead the Seminoles to wins against rivals Florida Gators in both teams' home stadiums.

WILLIE TAGGART Willie Taggart accepted the head coaching job at Florida State University at the end of 2017. Taggart made history when he joined the Seminoles. He is the first African American coach in the history of the team. Along with new energy, he brings a record of success to the team. He previously coached at the University of Oregon and left that team with a winning season.

The Mascot

The student who portrays Osceola is carefully selected by the university. He must maintain a 3.0 grade point average (GPA) and learn to ride a horse bareback. He must also commit to up to 30 hours of practice a week and exhibit respect for the role as a symbol of the Seminole people.

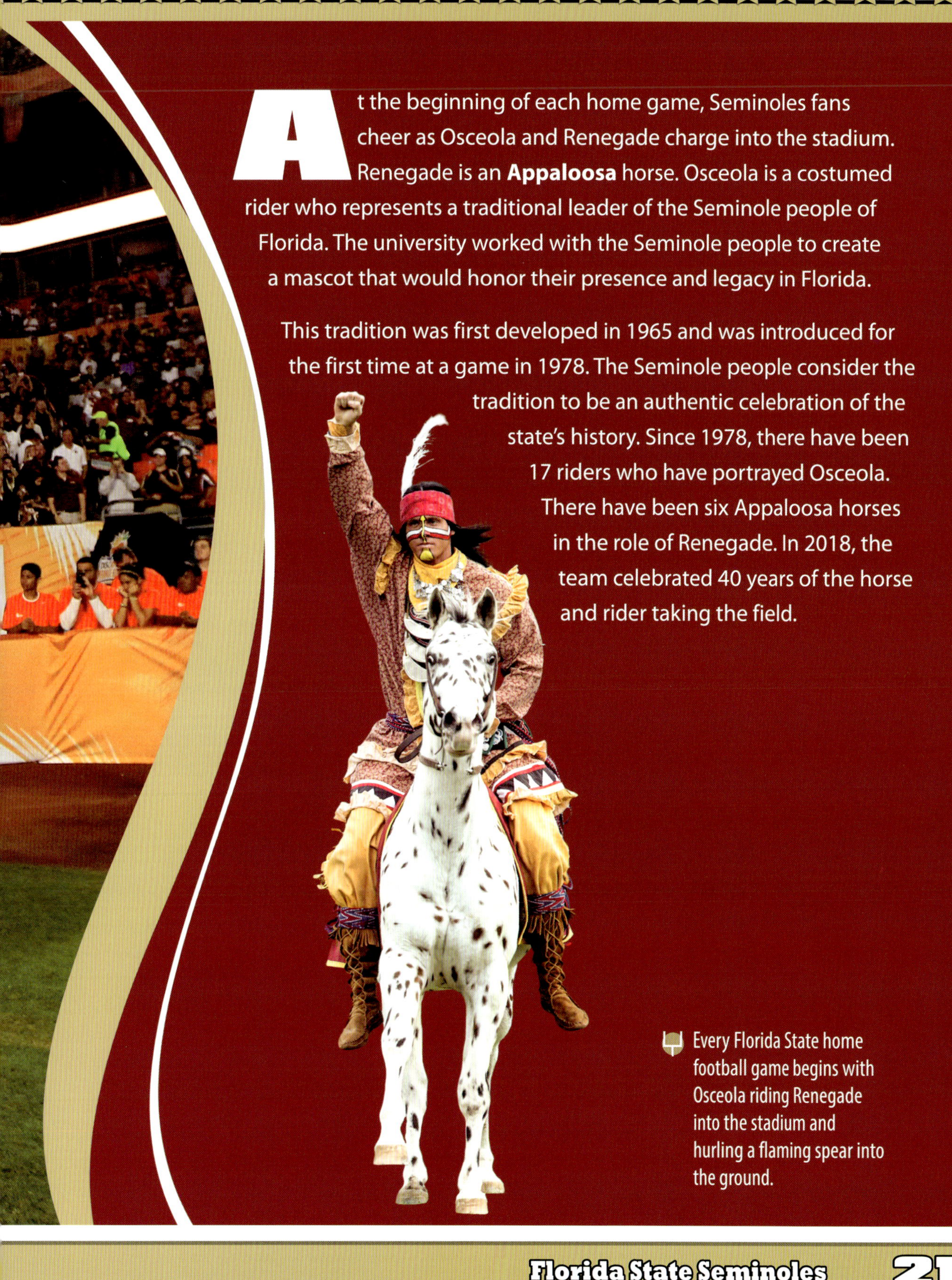

At the beginning of each home game, Seminoles fans cheer as Osceola and Renegade charge into the stadium. Renegade is an **Appaloosa** horse. Osceola is a costumed rider who represents a traditional leader of the Seminole people of Florida. The university worked with the Seminole people to create a mascot that would honor their presence and legacy in Florida.

This tradition was first developed in 1965 and was introduced for the first time at a game in 1978. The Seminole people consider the tradition to be an authentic celebration of the state's history. Since 1978, there have been 17 riders who have portrayed Osceola. There have been six Appaloosa horses in the role of Renegade. In 2018, the team celebrated 40 years of the horse and rider taking the field.

Every Florida State home football game begins with Osceola riding Renegade into the stadium and hurling a flaming spear into the ground.

Legends of the Past

For many players, their time with the Seminoles is the start of a promising football career. These are some of the best-known football players to play at Florida State.

Xavier Rhodes

Xavier Rhodes played for Florida State University from 2009 to 2012. During the 2010 season, he started in all 14 games. In his college career, he started in a total of 38 out of 43 games. During his junior year, Rhodes was a finalist for the Jim Thorpe Award, which is awarded to the top defensive receiver in college football. Rhodes was well-known for leading a strong defensive team for the Seminoles. He was selected in the first round of the NFL **draft** in 2013 by the Minnesota Vikings.

Position: Cornerback
Seasons: 2009–2012 (Florida State Seminoles), 2013–Present (Minnesota Vikings)
Born: June 19, 1990, Miami, Florida

Devonta Freeman

During his three seasons at Florida State, Devonta Freeman was a key part of the Seminoles' running game. Most seasons Freeman played, he was the team leader in rushing yards. This commitment paid off in his junior year. In 2013, he rushed a total of 1,016 yards. This was a career high for Freeman. This season also marked a 10-game streak, during which Freeman made a rushing touchdown in each game. Freeman entered the 2014 NFL draft after his junior year and was selected by the Atlanta Falcons. Freeman signed a five-year contract with the Falcons in 2017.

Position: Running Back
Seasons: 2011–2013 (Florida State Seminoles), 2014–Present (Atlanta Falcons)
Born: March 15, 1992, Baxley, Georgia

Lamarcus Joyner

Lamarcus Joyner ended his high school football career as the number-one cornerback prospect in the country. Despite many offers from schools across the country, Joyner chose to stay in his home state and play for the Seminoles. As a freshman, he started every game, a rare honor for first-year players. Joyner would continue to start in most games during his time in Tallahassee. As a junior, he was a starter at the safety position. He had 69 tackles in his last year at Florida State. He was also nominated for the Thorpe Award. In the second round of the 2014 NFL draft, Joyner was selected by the St. Louis Rams, which later moved to Los Angeles.

Position: Free Safety
Seasons: 2010–2013 (Florida State Seminoles), 2014–Present (St. Louis/Los Angeles Rams)
Born: November 27, 1990, Miami, Florida

Rodney Hudson

Rodney Hudson played for the Florida State Seminoles for all four years of his college career. By the time he was picked in the 2011 NFL draft, he was the most-honored offensive lineman that had ever played for the Seminoles. Hudson was listed as a final candidate for the Lombardi Award and the Outland Trophy. He was honored as part of the Freshman All-America first team. Hudson was also named a first-team All-American in 2010 during his senior year. Hudson spent four seasons with the Kansas City Chiefs before transferring to the Oakland Raiders in 2015, where he still plays.

Position: Center
Seasons: 2007–2010 (Florida State Seminoles), 2011–2014 (Kansas City Chiefs), 2015–Present (Oakland Raiders)
Born: July 12, 1989, Mobile, Alabama

All-Time Records

34

Single-Game Rushes

In August 1998, Travis Minor set the Seminoles record for most rushes in a single game, with 34.

11

Single-Game Touchdowns

In a 2017 game against Delaware State University, the Seminoles made 11 touchdowns, the most in a single game in their history.

723

Single-Season Points

In 2013, FSU scored a total of 723 points, setting the all-time record for the team.

43

Most Consecutive Games with a Pass Reception

Between 2011 and 2014, Rashad Greene set the Seminoles' record of 43 consecutive games catching a pass.

29

Highest Margin of Victory in a Bowl Game

The highest margin of victory for the Seminoles in a bowl game is 29 points, which they achieved in both 2008 and 2017.

Timeline

Throughout the team's history, the Florida State Seminoles have had many memorable events that have become defining moments for the team and its fans.

1947
After WWII, college football gains popularity. FSU creates the Florida Seminoles with Ed Williamson as head coach.

1964
Under the guidance of Coach Peterson, the Seminoles beat their rival the Florida Gators for the first time.

1900 | 1920 | 1940 | 1960

In 1902, the first college football team in Tallahassee, Florida, takes the field. This team is known as the Eleven.

1960
Bill Peterson takes the role of head coach for the Florida Seminoles.

1976
Bobby Bowden joins the Florida Seminoles as head coach after he leaves his coaching position in West Virginia.

The Future
During the Bobby Bowden era of Seminoles history, fans enjoyed many winning seasons and high rankings. Each team and coach since then has worked to build on those successes. Coach Taggart is looking ahead and hoping to continue the Seminole traditions of winning and excelling in the regular season, as well as the postseason.

1990s
Coach Bowden leads his team to a successful run in the 1990s, boasting an 88-percent winning percentage.

1980

2000

2020

In 1994, FSU battles back against a 29-point lead held by rival Florida Gators to tie the game known as "the Choke at Doak," 31–31.

2010
Jimbo Fisher takes over as the ninth head coach for FSU.

2001
The Florida Seminoles' record winning streak ends, marking the 14th consecutive season the team has had 10 or more wins.

2017
The Seminoles begin a new era of football with Coach Willie Taggart at the end of the 2017 season.

Write a Biography

Life Story

A person's life story can be the subject of a book. This kind of book is called a biography. Biographies often describe the lives of people who have achieved great success. These people may be alive today, or they may have lived many years ago. Reading a biography can help you learn more about a great person.

Get the Facts

Use this book, and research in the library and on the internet, to find out more about your favorite player. Learn as much about him as you can. What position does he play? What are his statistics in important categories? Has he set any records? Also, be sure to write down key events in the person's life. What was his childhood like? What has he accomplished off the field? Is there anything else that makes this person special or unusual?

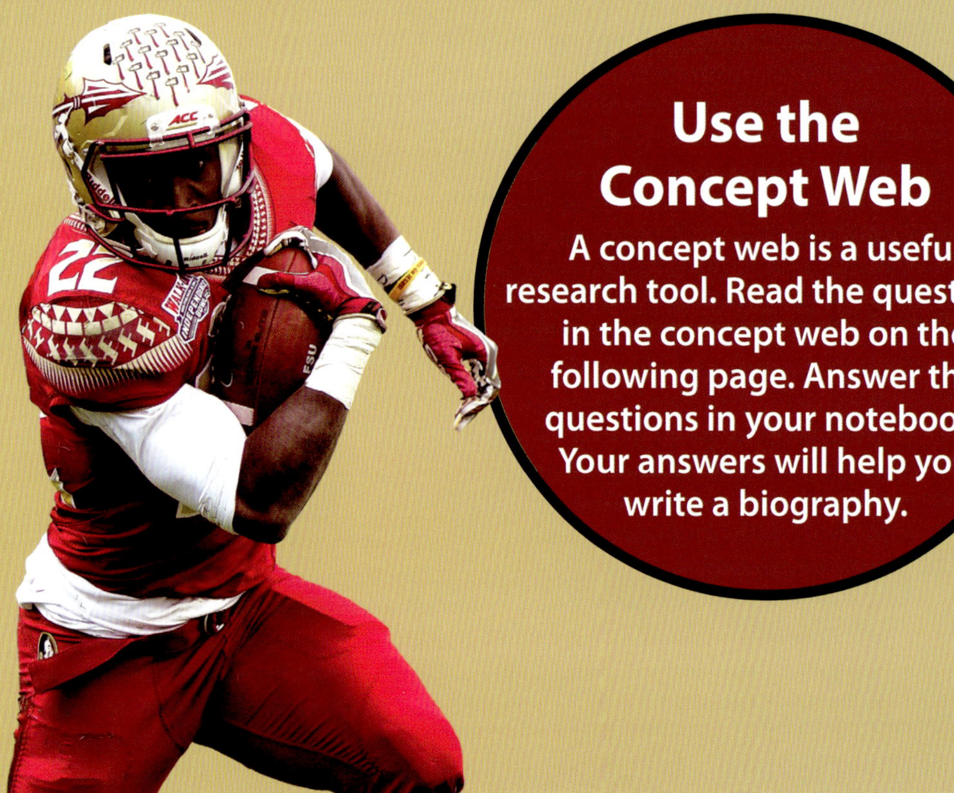

Use the Concept Web

A concept web is a useful research tool. Read the questions in the concept web on the following page. Answer the questions in your notebook. Your answers will help you write a biography.

Concept Web

Adulthood

- Where does this individual currently reside?
- Does he have a family?

Your Opinion

- What did you learn from the books you read in your research?
- Would you suggest these books to others?
- Was anything missing from these books?

Childhood

- Where and when was this person born?
- Describe his parents, siblings, and friends.
- Did this person grow up in unusual circumstances?

Accomplishments off the Field

- What is this person's life's work?
- Has he received awards or recognition for accomplishments?
- How have this person's accomplishments served others?

Write a Biography

Help and Obstacles

- Did this individual have a positive attitude?
- Did he receive help from others?
- Did this person have a mentor?
- Did this person face any hardships?
- If so, how were the hardships overcome?

Accomplishments on the Field

- What records does this person hold?
- What key games and plays have defined his career?
- What are his stats in categories important to his position?

Work and Preparation

- What was this person's education?
- What was his work experience?
- How does this person work?
- What is the process he uses?

Trivia Time

Take this quiz to test your knowledge of the Florida State Seminoles. The answers are printed upside down under each question.

1 Who are the Seminoles' biggest rivals?

A. The Miami Hurricanes and the Florida State Gators

2 What year was the Florida State Seminoles' first season?

A. 1947

3 How many home stadiums have the Seminoles had?

A. Two

4 Where do the Seminoles play?

A. Doak Campbell Stadium

5 Who is the Seminoles' current head coach?

A. Willie Taggart

6 How many All-American players have the Seminoles had?

A. 218

7 Who was the winningest coach in the Seminoles' history?

A. Bobby Bowden

8 What is the stadium's nickname?

A. "The house that Bobby built"

9 What are the Seminoles' colors?

A. Garnet and gold

10 What movie and television star once played for Florida State?

A. Burt Reynolds

Key Words

All-Americans: players, usually in high school or college, judged to be the best in each position of a sport

Appaloosa: a horse from North America with dark spots on light hair

draft: an annual event where the NFL chooses college football players to be new team members

Fred Biletnikoff Award: an award given to the best receiver in college football

Heisman Memorial Trophy: an annual award given to the college football player who best demonstrates excellence and hard work

off-season: a time of year when a specific sport or activity is not played

postseason: a sporting event that takes place after the end of the regular season

prospective: a player who is likely to succeed in a sport at a high level

renovation: construction that works to improve or expand an older building

rivals: groups or individuals who compete toward the same objective or goal

vacated: to cancel or give up something

Index

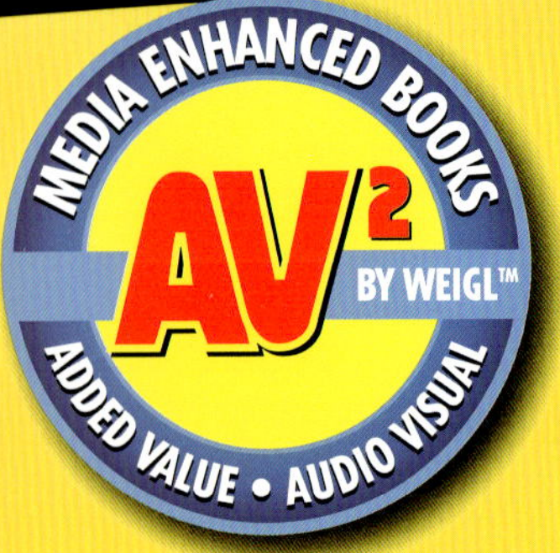

Log on to www.av2books.com

AV² by Weigl brings you media enhanced books that support active learning. Go to www.av2books.com, and enter the special code found on page 2 of this book. You will gain access to enriched and enhanced content that supplements and complements this book. Content includes video, audio, weblinks, quizzes, a slideshow, and activities.

AV² Online Navigation

Audio
Listen to sections of the book read aloud.

Book Pages
AV² pages directly correspond to pages in the book.

Video
Watch informative video clips.

Embedded Weblinks
Gain additional information for research.

Key Words
Study vocabulary, and complete a matching word activity.

Try This!
Complete activities and hands-on experiments.

Quizzes
Test your knowledge.

Slideshow
View images and captions, and prepare a presentation.

AV² was built to bridge the gap between print and digital. We encourage you to tell us what you like and what you want to see in the future.

Sign up to be an AV² Ambassador at www.av2books.com/ambassador.

Due to the dynamic nature of the internet, some of the URLs and activities provided as part of AV² by Weigl may have changed or ceased to exist. AV² by Weigl accepts no responsibility for any such changes. All media enhanced books are regularly monitored to update addresses and sites in a timely manner. Contact AV² by Weigl at 1-866-649-3445 or av2books@weigl.com with any questions, comments, or feedback.